Mastering Real Estate

Boosting Wealth Through Smart Property Investments

Table of Contents

Chapter 1. Introduction

Welcome to our Special Report on "Mastering Real Estate: Boosting Wealth Through Smart Property Investments"! If you have ever pondered the idea of venturing into real estate, this report is a golden opportunity, ready to unmask every secret in property investing. It shines a light on proven tactics, tips, and sound strategies smartly crafted by professionals to catapult your wealth to staggering new heights! Not teeming with overly technical jargon, this report is your cheerful companion that breaks down complex elements into easily digestible bits. It's like having a knowledgeable friend guide you through the journey. Prepare to get excited about real estate investments like never before, and see how this report is a ticket to your fortune!

Chapter 2. Unlocking the Potential of Property Investment

As an admired career with countless fruitful opportunities, property investment stands as a fortress embodying the potential to generate ample wealth. To reap its benefits, understanding its comprehensive scope is crucial. This chapter will focus on the art of evaluating the potential of property investments and the steps to strategize your venture.

2.1. Understanding the Market

The initial step is to develop an understanding of the real estate market. Real estate markets can fluctuate depending on several factors. Keeping an eye on housing trends, economic indicators, and mortgage rates will provide valuable insight into which way the market might swing.

Economic indicators can reveal which markets are thriving and which are not. Pay close attention to market rates for rentals, home prices, the average number of days on the market, and the percentage of rentals versus homeowners in a particular area. Collecting this data allows you to see patterns and anticipate future trends.

2.2. Researching Lucrative Locations

In property investment, location remains paramount. For profitable investments, diligent research into locations is necessary. Consider the population growth, job opportunities, and infrastructure plans of a region. A growing population and booming job market can lead to increased demand for property. Additionally, areas with plans for infrastructure development can be perfect for investment since property values are predicted to increase.

2.3. Investment Property Types

As an investor, it is essential to understand the types of properties that can generate returns. Residential properties are a popular choice due to the consistent demand for housing. However, commercial properties can also be lucrative. They can generate higher returns, although they might demand more investment.

Vacation rentals have been increasingly profitable, especially with the advent of platforms like Airbnb. On the other hand, industrial real estate like warehouses and factories have potential. Property types should be chosen depending on the market, location, and your personal capabilities and resources.

2.4. Calculating the Costs

A foundational step is to calculate the potential costs and returns of a prospective property. Costs can be divided into acquisition costs (purchasing the property) and holding costs (monthly expenses). Meanwhile, returns can be measured through rental income and appreciating property value.

Estimating costs can be complex. Take into account factors like mortgage payments, maintenance costs, property taxes, and potential property management costs. Comparing this to the potential income from renters, consider if the deal is worthwhile.

2.5. Risk Assessment

Investing in real estate comes with varied risks. It is critical to be aware and prepared. Market volatility, tenant issues, natural disasters, property damage, and legal troubles are potential problems. Insurance is a method to manage these risks. Always perform a risk assessment before purchasing a property, noting the factors you have control over and those out of your control.

2.6. Refurbishing and Improving Properties

Property improvement is an effective way to elevate the asset's value. Whether it is for renting or selling, refurbishing can attract more potential tenants or buyers. Common improvements include modernizing the kitchen and bathroom, landscaping the garden, and repainting the interiors.

Bear in mind, though, improvements should be cost-efficient. It might not prove profitable spending exorbitant amounts on renovations that won't considerably increase the property's value. Always weigh the costs against potential benefits.

2.7. Property Management

In property investing, management is an inevitable role. It includes the maintenance of the property, catering to tenant needs, policies, rules, contracts, and rent collection. For multiple properties, this can become a complex task.

While managing your properties can save costs, hiring a property management company could be a smart choice to save time and avoid complications. They handle tenant needs, collect rent, and manage the maintenance tasks, freeing you from everyday hassles.

By assimilating knowledge and implementing intelligent strategies, property investment can be a prosperous journey. Ensure to conduct thorough research, be patient, and stay updated about the latest real estate trends. Remember, time is a crucial factor in property appreciation. Patience, along with the right steps, can help you unlock the immense potential of property investment.

Chapter 3. The Anatomy of the Real Estate Market

This chapter aims to dissect, analyze, and essentially understand the workings of the Real Estate Market. The real estate market is a complex aggregation of buyers and sellers with diverse motivations and characteristics. It's not a single, homogenous entity but a patchwork of submarkets, each with its own nuances. Stepping into this labyrinth can be intimidating, but our in-depth exploration will ensure you navigate it with ease.

3.1. CORE CONCEPTS OF REAL ESTATE MARKET

The first step to mastering real estate investments is understanding its core concepts. The real estate market is influenced not only by the usual economic factors such as demand and supply but also by less tangible elements like location, buyer and seller psychology, and government regulations.

1. Demand and Supply: The bedrock principles of any market, demand reflects the buyer's willingness and ability to purchase, and supply represents the seller's willingness and ability to sell. In real estate, demand often outstrips supply, leading to rising prices. However, it's important to remember that the reverse can also occur.

2. Location: Location plays a pivotal role in the real estate market. The location's desirability, influenced by factors like amenities, infrastructure, and employment opportunities, significantly impacts property values.

3. Market Participants: The real estate market includes buyers, sellers, investors, renters, and intermediaries such as brokers

and agents. Each participant influences the market dynamics.

4. Government Regulations: These can alter market dynamics, create or diminish opportunities, and impact the cost of properties.

5. Investment Strategies: From flipping houses to rental properties, various strategies can be employed based on buyers' financial resources, risk tolerance, and market knowledge.

3.2. UNDERSTANDING THE CYCLES

The real estate market goes through four distinct phases, each presenting unique opportunities and challenges for investors.

1. Expansion: This is when demand exceeds supply, and new construction starts. Property prices rise during this phase.

2. Oversupply: Supply catches up with demand and surpasses it. Prices stabilize and may start to decline.

3. Recession: Oversupply continues as demand diminishes. Property prices decline further.

4. Recovery: Demand starts to pick up, but supply may not increase immediately. Prices stabilize and may begin to increase.

Understanding these cycles equips investors to time their purchases and sales to maximize returns.

3.3. REGIONAL VARIATIONS

The phrase, "All real estate is local," encapsulates the essential characteristic of the real estate market: its susceptibility to regional variations. Factors affecting a property in New York can be entirely different from those affecting one in San Francisco.

Understanding local factors, including job growth, population trends, local government regulations, and the area's economic health, helps investors make informed decisions. Spend time researching the local market, speaking with area experts, observing trends, and analyzing data. This due diligence can significantly improve investment outcomes.

3.4. EVALUATING THE MARKETS

Accurate evaluation of real estate markets is vital. Markets can differ significantly based on the type of property involved, such as residential, commercial, or industrial, and the geographical location.

A successful evaluation begins with extensive research, followed by in-depth analysis of the data gathered. Factors to consider include: - Market trends: Is the area growing, stagnant, or declining? - Employment statistics: Is job growth strong? What are the primary industries? - Demographics: What is the area's population, and what trends are evident in terms of age, income, and family composition? - Property values and rental rates: Are they rising, stable, or declining?

3.5. STRATEGIES FOR SUCCESS

With a fair understanding of the real estate market, it's now time to consider strategies for success. Here's where your comprehension of the market dynamics comes into play.

1. Diversification: Investing in different types of properties and/or different geographical locations can dilute risk.

2. Leveraging: This involves using borrowed capital for an investment, expecting the profits made to be higher than the interest payable.

3. Buy and Hold: A long-term strategy, this involves buying properties and holding them for an extended period.

4. Fix and Flip: This strategy involves buying underpriced or

distressed properties, renovating, and selling them at a profit.

Understanding these strategies helps align your investments with your financial goals and risk tolerance levels. Be informed, stay patient, monitor your investments continuously, and be ready to react to market changes.

The real estate market, with its complexities and dynamics, has the potential to offer substantial returns. A deep awareness of its structure and functioning will enable you to make informed investment decisions that can boost your wealth and secure your financial future.

Chapter 4. Investment Properties Demystified

Investment properties can seem like quite a convoluted concept at the surface, especially for first-time investors. But, in essence, it's about understanding the diversity of options available, analysing their potential for profit, and taking a calculated risk.

4.1. Understanding the Concept

An investment property is essentially a real estate asset purchased with the primary intention of gaining a return on the investment. This could be either through the resale of the property in the future, rental income, or both. They can be any type of property, including residential, commercial, and industrial.

It's important to mention that buying a home to live in does not classify as an investment property. The purpose here is not to gain a return, but to provide shelter instead. A property becomes an investment when the financial benefits become the primary focus.

4.2. The Types of Investment Properties

There are a few common types of investment properties you'll likely come across on your journey.

1. Residential Properties: These encompass anything from a single-family house to a condominium or townhome that you rent out. Lofts, duplexes, triplexes, and fourplexes are also part of residential properties. The profits in these cases come from rental income or the property's value appreciating over time.

2. Commercial Properties: These include business offices, shopping centres, and retail buildings. Here, the tenant usually signs a long-term lease, often for years, ensuring a steady cash flow for you, the owner.

3. Industrial Properties: Including warehouses, garages, distribution centres, and manufacturing factories. These investments usually demand a large amount of capital but offer a considerable potential for returns.

4. Mixed-use Properties: As the name suggests, these properties combine any of the above types. An example could be a building with retail shops on the ground floor and residential apartments on the upper floors.

4.3. Choosing the Right Investment Property

Deciding on the type of property you want to invest in is only the first step. Following that, you have to ensure that the property you choose is the right one and will indeed earn you profits.

A crucial factor to consider is the location. An ideal location is one that is attractive to potential tenants or buyers depending on your strategy. Some factors that make a particular location ideal include high employment rates, good transport connections, schools, amenities, low crime rates, and future growth prospects.

Also, consider the property's market value and how it is likely to appreciate or depreciate. Check similar properties in the area to get an approximate idea. Alternatively, you can hire a real estate appraiser for a more accurate valuation.

Do not forget about maintenance costs. A property might seem like a great deal, but if it requires extensive repairs, the costs can eat into your profits. Always get a property inspected before purchasing.

4.4. Financing Your Property

Contrary to what some might think, buying a property outrightly isn't the only option. Financing your property is quite common in the world of real estate investment.

Mortgages are the most common form of financing. You borrow money from a bank or another lender and pay it back over a specified time with interest. If you default on the loan, the lender can take over the property. Before you apply for a mortgage, ensure that your credit history is clean and healthy.

There's also an option of partnering with someone else to finance your property. In real estate investment terms, this is known as syndication. The partner can be a friend, family, or even another investor.

Then you have hard money lenders. These are individuals or companies who lend money to investors at high interest rates and short repayment times. They make loans based on the value of the property instead of the borrower's creditworthiness. This is a popular option among those who plan on flipping properties.

Investment properties can be confusing at first. But, once you understand what they are, how to choose the right one, and the various ways to finance them, the path becomes clearer. Remember, every step you take towards mastering real estate is a step closer towards boosting your wealth.

Chapter 5. Crucial Tips for First-Time Investors

While contemplating your first property investment, it's essential to dig through a mound of information, consider a cascade of factors, and forge a solid arsenal of effective strategies. This chapter delves into several critical tips that will help novice investors navigate this exciting and complex world of real estate.

5.1. Know Your Financial Situation

Start by possessing an informed understanding of your financial standing. Reviewing your credit score, monthly income, expenditures, loans, and any other financial commitments is paramount. Once you paint the precise picture of your financial situation, you can then determine your readiness for real estate investment. Remember to factor in potential costs for repairs and maintenance when estimating your budget.

5.2. Save For Down Payment

Unlike a typical homeowner loan, investment properties often require a larger down payment—sometimes as much as 20-30%. Accordingly, diligent saving is a requisite for the initial investment. Cultivate a regular saving habit, cut down on unnecessary expenses, and refine your budget to meet this requirement.

5.3. Research and Understand the Market

The real world of real estate can be more complex than it seems on paper. Conduct a thorough market analysis considering fluctuations, property market trends, locales with promising investment returns, etc. Effectively predicting market trends based on historical data and current socio-economic factors can give you a decisive edge.

5.4. Choose the Right Property Type

Among residential, commercial, and industrial properties, each type offers a unique set of opportunities and risks. Identify which type aligns best with your financial goals, risk tolerance, and management style. This step will also aid in refining your search and saving time.

5.5. Location, Location, Location

Few factors influence property value and rental income potential as much as location. Reiterating the time-tested mantra, a prime location ensures long-term capital gains. Proximity to necessities such as schools, healthcare centers, supermarkets, and transportation links can significantly increase a property's attractiveness.

5.6. Build a Reliable Network

Foster strong relationships with real estate professionals - be it agents, other investors, attorneys, or financial advisors. They are an abundant source of valuable insights, advice, and potential deals.

5.7. Inspect Thoroughly

Once you've identified a prospect, an exhaustive property inspection is imperative. Look out for any potential issues—structural damage, ancient plumbing, outdated wiring, etc. Consider hiring a professional home inspection service if necessary.

5.8. Have an Exit Strategy

Unpredictability is a badge of life, and real estate investments are no exception. Having an exit strategy in hand equips you to deal with sudden twists and turns. Whether it's selling the property or converting it into a rental, your exit strategy should align with your broader investment goals and market trends.

5.9. Refrain from Expecting Overnight Success

Real estate investment is not a get-rich-quick scheme. It requires patience, diligence, resilience, and smart strategy. Respect the process and give your investment the time it needs to prosper.

5.10. Understand the Tax Implications

Understanding tax laws related to property investments can help you save money and avoid potential legal issues. Consult with a certified accountant or tax lawyer to clearly understand tax deductions, the impact of rental income on your tax slab, capital gains tax, and more.

5.11. Stay Committed to Continuous Learning

Last but far from least, foster an insatiable desire to learn. Real estate markets are dynamic; the learning curve never really ends. Regularly updated knowledge helps you make informed decisions and seize new opportunities.

By adhering to the tips and strategies detailed above, the path to mastering the art and science of real estate investment becomes an attainable, rewarding journey. Coupled with an intricate understanding of market dynamics, impeccable timing, and an ever-ready learning mindset, you will see your wealth grow in leaps and bounds through smart property investments.

Chapter 6. Property Portfolio Management: Strategies for Success

Every property investment starts with one enduring vision: to grow a robust portfolio that not only creates passive income but also paves the way for a wealthy future. This part of the guide will be your ultimate companion, unraveling practical insights, as well as strategies to secure sustainable success in your property portfolio management.

6.1. Understanding Property Portfolio Management

Diversification is a critical mantra in the world of investment. It means spreading your investments across different assets to minimize risk. In simple words, don't put all your eggs in one basket. Property is one such asset class that offers diversification, inflation protection, and a stable source of income—three crucial components of sound investment.

Your property portfolio can include a variety of investment types: residential real estate (apartments, houses, multi-family units), commercial real estate (offices, retail shops, warehouses), and indirect property investments (Real Estate Investment Trusts [REITs]).

Managing a property portfolio isn't just about owning numerous properties. It's about effectively managing those properties to ensure they provide regular income, appreciate in value, and reduce taxation. This requires analyzing market trends, regularly reviewing property performance, fine-tuning your investment strategy, and making decisions about buying, selling, or holding specific investments.

6.2. Building a Robust Property Portfolio

As an aspiring property mogul, your initial steps should focus on creating a robust property portfolio that generates a steady income stream and appreciates over time. Here are some steps you can take:

1. Understand your financial capability: Know what you can afford. Make sure you have enough savings for down payments and enough income to cover any loan repayments and property maintenance.

2. Diversify: Don't just invest in one type of property or location. Diversify across different types of properties and locations to spread risk.

3. Seek professional advice: Professional property advisors can provide you with insights on where and when to invest based on your financial situation and goals.

4. Regularly review: Set a timeline to review your property portfolio regularly. This will help you make informed decisions about whether to hold, sell or buy more properties.

6.3. Streamlining processes

As your portfolio grows, managing all the properties can become a demanding task: dealing with tenants, handling maintenance requests, tracking rental payments, dealing with vacancies, etc. Here, implementing a streamlined process for handling these tasks is vital.

You can consider property management software, which allows you to centralize all property information, track rent payments, handle maintenance requests, and more. Alternatively, you might want to hire a property management company, especially if you have a lot of properties or they are spread out geographically.

6.4. Risk Management

With any investment, there's always an element of risk involved. For property investments, the risks could be property damage, vacancies, market downturns, or increases in interest rates. Understanding and mitigating these risks are key facets of successful property investment.

One essential risk management strategy is diversification: investing in different property types and varying locations. This can protect your portfolio against downturns in any one property market.

Getting insurance is another essential risk management strategy. Property insurance typically covers damage to the property from certain events, such as fires or natural disasters. Depending on your policy, it could also provide income protection in case of vacancies.

6.5. Optimizing for Tax Efficiency

Property investment offers several tax benefits that smart investors take advantage of. Mortgage interest, property taxes, operating expenses, depreciation, and even certain travel expenses can be tax-deductible.

It's important to carefully track and document all your property-related expenses. Use software to help keep track of these expenses and consult with a tax advisor to ensure you're fully leveraging tax benefits.

6.6. Reviewing and Improving your Portfolio

Reviewing your portfolio regularly is crucial. This involves evaluating each property's performance, assessing your overall return on investment, and understanding how market trends might impact your portfolio.

It's important to remember that investment isn't a static process. Your goals may change over time. Market dynamics may change. Therefore, your investment strategy should be flexible enough to accommodate these changes. Be ready to pivot when needed, whether that means selling a property, buying more, or venturing into a new market.

In conclusion, property portfolio management is a multifaceted discipline that requires savvy strategic planning, ongoing review, and the flexibility to adapt as your circumstances and market conditions change. Done correctly, it can generate substantial streams of income and serve as a significant wealth-creation vehicle. The journey might be long and requires work, but the rewards can definitely be worth the effort.

Chapter 7. Real Estate Valuation: Spotting the Diamond in the Rough

Real estate valuation is arguably one of the most critical aspects of successful property investing. By mastering the art of property valuation, you can identify undervalued properties, assess potential returns, and secure lucrative deals.

7.1. Understanding the Basics

Real estate valuation refers to the process of estimating a property's worth in the current market. Several factors and methods can influence the valuation.

Two crucial terms in real estate valuation are Market Value and Intrinsic Value. Market value is what people are willing to pay for a property on the open market. Intrinsic value, on the other hand, is the property's true value, considering all factors such as location, size, condition, and the local real estate market.

7.2. Valuation Methods

Here are the main methods for property valuation:

1. Sales Comparisons Approach: This method compares features of the subject property with recently sold properties with similar attributes in the same area.

2. Cost Approach: This method takes into account the cost to reproduce or replace a property (replacement cost), minus any depreciation.

3. Income Capitalization Approach: This technique estimates a property's value based on the income it is expected to generate in the future.

7.3. Sales Comparison Approach: The Details

The Sales Comparison Approach (SCA) is most used in residential real estate. It is based on the premise that like properties will sell for like prices. The similarity is typically based on features such as location, square footage, the number of rooms, and property condition.

The SCA involves five steps:

1. Identify Comparable Properties: Look for recent sales of similar properties.

2. Adjust for Differences: Make adjustments for major differences between the comparable property and your property.

3. Weigh the Comparable Properties: Give more weight to the more similar properties.

4. Calculate the Average Price Per Unit: This could be square footage, per room, or another metric.

5. Multiply the Unit Price by Your Property's Units: Use the average price per unit to estimate the value of the property.

7.4. Cost Approach: The Details

The Cost Approach (CA) is commonly used for unique properties or new construction. Here's how it works:

1. Determine Land Value: This can be obtained from sales data for nearby vacant land.

2. Calculate Replacement Cost: The cost to recreate a like building at

current material and labor costs.

3. Estimate Depreciation: Take into account all forms of physical wear and tear or functional obsolescence.

4. Add the Land Value to The Replacement Cost: Just remember to subtract the depreciation.

7.5. Income Capitalization Approach: The Details

The Income Capitalization Approach (ICA) is used mainly for commercial property valuation. It estimates the value of a property based on the income it generates. Here's a simplified procedure:

1. Determine Annual Gross Income: The total income from rents or leases.

2. Subtract Operating Expenses: Include taxes, insurance, and maintenance.

3. Apply The Capitalization Rate: This is used to estimate the investor's potential return on their investment.

7.6. Factors Affecting Property Value

Many factors can affect a property's value. While some are fixed, like the location, others may change over time, like the local market conditions.

1. Location: Proximity to amenities, the quality of local schools, and commute distance.

2. Neighborhood: Look at the condition of neighboring properties, local crime rates, and general upkeep.

3. Age and Condition: Older properties may need significant upkeep. Condition can also significantly affect a property's value.

4. Market Conditions: Housing supply and demand, interest rates, and the economy as a whole.

7.7. Learning to Spot the 'Diamond in the Rough'

Properties with high potential but currently in a poor state are often referred to as 'diamonds in the rough.' Recognizing these can be a goldmine for savvy investors. Often, these properties may be undervalued due to cosmetic disrepair, outdated features, or minor structural issues – all of which can be remedied with a bit of work and investment.

Key attributes to look for in these properties are:

1. Great Location: Even in a less desirable state, properties in prime locations always carry potential.

2. Solid Structure: Look for properties with safe and strong underlying structures.

3. Cosmetic Issues: These are less expensive to fix but can significantly boost a property's value.

4. Positive Cash Flow Potential: The property should have the potential to attract tenants if it's intended for rental use.

By carefully assessing potential investments using the valuation methods detailed above and considering the important valuation factors, investors can confidently spot undervalued properties or 'diamonds in the rough. This, combined with the right location, due diligence, market understanding, and good timing, can indeed set the stage for significant returns in the realm of property investments.

Chapter 8. Risk Assessment and Mitigation in Property Investments

Real estate, like any other form of investment, carries its share of risks. However, these risks need not dissuade investors from pursuing opportunities in this sector. Instead, they should prompt a thorough, strategic focus on risk assessment and mitigation. The purpose of this section is to equip investors with the requisite knowledge to accurately gauge risks and formulate strategies to reduce their impact.

8.1. Understanding Risks in Property Investments

At the core of successful property investment is the understanding of risks associated. These risks could range from changes in market conditions, legal complications, financial constraints to natural disasters. Identifying and understanding these risks are the first stepping stones on the path to risk mitigation.

1. Market Risks: Market conditions fluctuate due to varying economic circumstances such as inflation rates, interest rates, and unemployment figures. Property prices are significantly impacted by these changes. As an investor, one must have a solid grasp of the economic indicators and market trends.

2. Legal Risks: These encompass potential legal complications linked with property ownership, rentals, zoning laws, and tenant rights. Ignorance or oversight of any of these aspects could lead to financial losses or legal disputes.

3. Financial Risks: Risk tied to the ability to meet financial

obligations such as mortgage payments. Factors such as personal financial status, changes in interest rates, and loan terms come into play here.

4. Environmental Risks: These could result from natural disasters as well as man-made calamities, potentially causing significant damage to property.

8.2. Tools for Risk Assesment

Understanding risks is good, but assessing them with proven tools and methodologies can add further depth to your risk analysis. There are several tools and techniques available for the investors.

1. SWOT Analysis: Widely used across different sectors, SWOT (Strengths, Weaknesses, Opportunities, Threats) analysis provides an overall view of where a particular investment stands.

2. PEST Analysis: Political, Economic, Social, and Technological (PEST) analysis offers insights into the broader macro-environment in which the property exists. It's instrumental for evaluating market growth or decline.

3. Risk Matrix: A risk matrix classifies risks based on their likelihood of occurrence and the potential impact they would have on the investment. It aids in prioritizing the risks and formulating an appropriate response.

8.3. Evaluating Risk Vs Reward

Your risk tolerance levels determine the type of property investments you are comfortable with. Risk and reward typically have a direct relationship - higher the potential returns, higher the risk, and vice versa. It's critical to align investment decisions with personal risk tolerance levels to avoid undue panic or worry.

8.4. Mitigation Strategies

Once you've assessed the potential investment's risks, it's time to formulate mitigation strategies. Here are several effective tactics used by seasoned investors:

1. Diversification: Spread your investments across different types of properties and areas to omit the risk associated with a single market or sector.

2. Adequate Insurance: Insurance is essential in mitigating environmental and financial risks. It serves as a protective shield against unforeseen circumstances that could inflict financial losses.

3. Leverage Legal Advice: Engaging legal professionals will ensure you stay informed about all legal obligations, rights, and potential legal risks associated with a property investment.

4. Regular Market Analysis: Remain updated on market trends and economic indicators. These provide a warning for potential market risks that could impact your investments adversely.

Remember, no investment is entirely risk-free. The key is to develop a well-thought-out risk assessment and mitigation plan, enabling you to make informed decisions. The potential gains from real estate investments are substantial for those who understand how to navigate through the choppy seas of risk. Armed with knowledge and tact, you're set to journey into the realm of property investing - with wisdom as your compass and strategy as your map.

Chapter 9. Understanding Real Estate Finance: From Mortgages to Cash Flow

Real estate finance is a critical element for any aspiring investor to grasp since it informs decisions ranging from properties to purchase, to funding methods, to eventual paths to profitability. Going from mortgages to managing cash flow is comparable to learning a new language, replete with its own lexicon and rules. But fear not! Just like picking up a new language, it starts with mastering the fundamentals and gradually adding more complex concepts.

9.1. Understanding Mortgages

Arguably, one of the first tools on a real-estate investor's financial toolkit is learning to comprehend the realm of mortgages. A mortgage, in very basic terms, is a loan taken out to buy property or land. The loan is 'secured' against the property's value until it is entirely paid off. If the borrower can't keep up with the repayments, the lender can repossess the returned property.

The typical lifespan of the mortgage is approximately 25 years, but the term can be shorter or longer. The loan amount is subject to interest, which means the borrower ends up paying more than they initially borrowed to acquire the property.

All potential investors must grasp the many types of mortgages available to them, as picking the right one can majorly influence your investment's profitability.

Fixed-Rate Mortgages are most favored due to the predictable monthly payments. The interest rate stays the same over an agreed period, making it easier for budgeting.

Meanwhile, Adjustable-Rate Mortgages (ARMs) start with a fixed interest rate for a set duration, then the rate adjusts periodically according to market fluctuations.

Interest-Only Mortgages allow a borrower to only pay the interest on the loan for a stipulated period, after which they start repaying the principal.

Finally, a Balloon Mortgage requires small payments for the loan term and a lump-sum payment at the end.

9.2. Mortgage Pre-Approval

Mortgage pre-approval is another valuable tool for property investors. This means lender gives a borrower a pre-approval for a specific loan amount. It shows sellers that you're a serious buyer with the financial backing to purchase their property. It's important to note, however, that pre-approval doesn't guarantee you will actually receive the loan.

9.3. Managing Cash Flow

Cash flow is the net amount of cash moving into and out of a business. In real estate investing, it's commonly defined as rental income minus property operating expenses (e.g., taxes, insurance, maintenance, and property management).

Positive cash flow means the property's income exceeds its expenses. This property would be profitable from an operational perspective. On the other hand, negative cash flow implies the property's expenses exceed its income.

In the realm of real estate investing, a desirable cash flow can make or break an investor's decision to buy a property.

To calculate cash flow, take the amount of rent you receive from a property and subtract all your expenses (excluding mortgage). If you have a positive number, then congratulations—you have positive cash flow!

9.4. Understanding Cash Flow Calculation

Consider an example: If you're receiving $1,500 in rent and you pay $200 in taxes, $50 in insurance, $200 in maintenance, and $100 in property management, your expenses total up to $550 per month. Subtract this from your $1,500 income, and you'd find yourself netting a handy $950 every month.

Keep in mind that regular expenditures will not be your only costs. It's always wise to budget for irregular but inevitable expenses, such as unexpected repairs or vacancies, by setting aside a portion of your income every month.

9.5. Leveraging Positive Cash Flow in Real Estate Investment

The magical outcome of managing positive cash flow is that it allows investors to leverage income and expand their investment horizons. Any surplus income can be used to pay down the principal on the mortgage, effectively allowing the investor to build equity in the property faster.

Positive cash flow also provides a safety net during economic downturns. In times of recession, when property values plummet, the ability to continue making a profit makes holding onto your property easier until values increase again.

Additionally, income from positive cash flow properties can be reinvested into other properties, starting an accumulative cycle of wealth generation. Hence, managing and achieving positive cash flow is an integral part of savvy real estate investing strategy.

9.6. Final Thoughts

Mastering real estate finance, exploring mortgages to efficient cash flow management, is essential for any investor. Ensuring positive cash flow and leveraging it appropriately can act as a stepping stone towards building substantial wealth. However, it takes knowledge, patience, and strategic planning to thoroughly navigate this financial wilderness. With a good understanding of the financing options available, and efficient management of cash flow, there's nothing stopping an inspired investor from reaping the ripe fruits of the real estate industry!

Chapter 10. The Power of Location: A Detailed Study

The power of location in real estate cannot be overstressed. We've all heard the phrase, "location, location, location"—and there's a reason it's the mantra of the industry. A good location can make a mediocre property shine, while a bad one can cast a negative light on an otherwise attractive unit. Understanding the value of location can be a key driver in your real estate investing success.

10.1. Importance of location

First and foremost, let's discuss why location is so critical in real estate investments. The property itself, regardless of how breathtakingly beautiful or architecturally distinct, holds only a portion of the spectrum that defines its worth. The true value of the asset is the inherent stature of its locale.

Location greatly influences the desirability and price of a property. A property in a well-sought-after neighborhood can command a higher price than a similar property in a less desirable area. Moreover, location also impacts the livelihood and lifestyle of the inhabitants. Facilities such as good schools, hospitals, public transportation, and local amenities like grocery stores, restaurants, and parks, as well as the crime rate and overall standard of living, play a major role in determining an area's demand.

10.2. Establishing Property Value

One of the critical aspects influenced by location is the property value. The objective location factors can overshadow the physical and individual characteristics of the property. A smaller house in a high-demand neighborhood could potentially be worth more than a larger house in an undesirable area.

Factors to consider when evaluating location for determining property value include economic aspects (job market, income levels, and economic health of the region), demographic trends, local amenities, and infrastructural developments. Monitoring these variables can provide insights on how the value of your property investment might fluctuate with time.

10.3. Convenience and Accessibility

The convenience and accessibility of amenities play an essential role in making a location appealing. Proximity to places of work, commerce, education, recreation, and essential services determine a location's convenience. In most urban environments, being near public transportation is a significant asset. In suburban areas, proximity to major roadways and good schools matter the most.

A property situated near a large employer or in a thriving job market will likely be more rentable and maintain its value better than one in an economically depressed area. Key amenities such as shopping centers, restaurants, parks, schools, and hospitals also correspond to desirability.

10.4. Safety Considerations

Safety and crime levels of a neighborhood significantly impact a property's value and its allure for potential renters or buyers. High crime rates can lead to lower property values, reduced rent prices, and higher vacancy rates. No matter how attractive a property may look, if it's in a neighborhood known for high crime rates, it may be challenging to find willing tenants or buyers.

When analyzing an area's safety, it's not only about examining crime rates, but also about considering environmental safety. For instance, does the area have a history of floods, wildfires, or other natural disasters? These elements can influence insurance premiums and overall desirability.

10.5. Future Trends and Growth

Savvy real estate investors don't just consider what a location is offering now, but also how it is projected to grow in the future. An area with positive growth projections will be more appealing to potential buyers and renters, and this demand can drive property values and rental rates upward.

When assessing future trends, look at factors such as proposed developments, population growth, job growth, and changes in demographics. If a significant planning application, such as a new shopping center, school, or large employer, is approved, it could have a significant impact on property values.

10.6. Tax and Regulatory Environment

Beyond the physical characteristics of a location, the tax and regulatory climate can also impact a real estate investment. Property taxes, landlord-tenant laws, and zoning regulations can vary greatly from one location to another. It's essential to fully understand the implications of these elements and factor them into your investment decisions.

High property taxes can eat into rental profits, while landlord-tenant laws that favor tenants over landlords can lead to potential legal issues. Meanwhile, zoning regulations can restrict how a property is used or limit potential upgrades.

By taking into account the power of location, even the smallest real estate investor can greatly improve their chances of success.

However, it is important to remember that while location is incredibly important, it should be only one factor among many in a well-researched and evaluated investment strategy.

Investing in real estate involves a significant amount of due diligence. Understanding the components uncovered in this chapter and how they integrate into your decision-making process will undoubtedly enrich your knowledge as an investor and augment the potential success of your property investments. Mix knowledge with acumen, sprinkle in patience, and you have a winning recipe for mastering real estate.

Chapter 11. Future Trends: Predicting and Profiting from Market Shifts

Understanding market trends and their potential impact upon the real estate sector is akin to reading the future. It allows investors to fine-tune their strategies and optimize for success. In this segment, you will learn about the factors that drive these trends, methodologies to predict them, and how to turn these predictions into lucrative investment opportunities.

11.1. The Driving Forces Behind Market Shifts

The real estate industry is no isolated island. It is interconnected with various other sectors and is influenced by socio-economic, demographic, technological, and environmental factors.

- Socio-Economic Factors: These factors include income levels, employment rates, interest rates, and economic development. Increased job opportunities often lead to demand in housing and vice versa. Also, fluctuating interest rates significantly affect mortgage costs, and in turn, real estate markets.

- Demographic Trends: Changes in population structures, such as aging demographics, urbanization rates, family sizes etc., profoundly impact the types of properties that are in demand.

- Technological Advancements: Innovation and technological breakthroughs shape the real estate market too. For instance, the rise of remote working could lead to greater demand in residential spaces equipped with home offices.

- Environmental Changes: Natural disasters, climate change, and sustainability initiatives also steer market trends, affecting the desirability of certain property types and locations.

11.2. Predicting Market Shifts

Given these driving forces, predicting market shifts isn't akin to fortune-telling, but a systematic process of data analysis. There are a plethora of data sources at your disposal such as real estate market reports, forecasts by major banks or real estate consulting firms, government economic outlooks, and statistics on employment and wages.

A few key indicators to look out for include past property price performance, future infrastructure developments, changes in job opportunities, and population increase or decrease in a specific region.

11.3. Turning Predictions into Profits

Turning these predictions into successful investments requires careful planning and strategic execution.

1. Diversification: Invest across different types of real estate to minimize the risk of total loss if one sector doesn't perform as predicted.

2. Forward Planning: Factor market trends into your real estate business plan. Use your predicted trends not only to choose where to invest but also decide on the right timing.

3. Market Timing: While it is impossible to perfectly time the market, smart investors enter when prices are reduced and exit when the valuation has significantly appreciated.

4. Exit Strategy: Knowing when and how to exit your investments is

as important as knowing when to enter. A comprehensive exit strategy that gauges market trends is crucial.

11.4. Future Trends to Watch

In the ever-changing real estate matrix, several trends are worth your attention.

- Sustainable Properties: With climate change taking center-stage worldwide, there is an escalating demand for eco-friendly, energy-efficient homes.

- Co-Living Spaces: As millennials and Gen Z become prominent players in the real estate market, there is a rise in demand for co-living spaces, particularly in urban areas.

- Technology in Real Estate: PropTech, or technology in real estate, is on the rise, with AI, VR, and smart home technologies changing the face of real estate.

- Remote Work: The COVID-19-induced remote work trend has led to a need for home office spaces, and we can expect communities designed with telecommuters in mind.

By following these guidelines and understanding the impactful role that market trends play in real estate, investors can exploit these shifts to their advantage and stand to increase not just their wealth, but their proficiency in mastering the sector. Predicting and profiting from market shifts may seem daunting at first, but with careful research, strategic planning, and a touch of patience, you can become adept at navigating through the evolving tides of the real estate market.